CONTENTS

Simply Charms

LARK CRAFTS
An Imprint of
Sterling Publishing Co., Inc.
New York

For more information on **LARK CRAFTS**,
visit our website at **WWW.LARKCRAFTS.COM.**

Published by Lark Crafts
An Imprint of Sterling Publishing Co., Inc.
387 Park Avenue South, New York, NY 10016

ISBN 978-1-4547-0025-8

First published in this format in 2011.

The material was previously published in the book *Beading with Charms* (ISBN 978-1-60059-019-1).

© 2007, Lark Crafts, an imprint of Sterling Publishing Co., Inc.; unless otherwise specified

Distributed in Canada by Sterling Publishing, c/o Canadian Manda Group, 165 Dufferin Street
Toronto, Ontario, Canada M6K 3H6

Distributed in the United Kingdom by GMC Distribution Services,
Castle Place, 166 High Street, Lewes, East Sussex, England BN7 1XU

Distributed in Australia by Capricorn Link (Australia) Pty Ltd., P.O. Box 704, Windsor, NSW 2756 Australia

TECHNIQUES

Before You Begin

One of the joys of making jewelry is choosing your supplies from the tremendous variety of beads, charms, findings, pearls, and types of wire that are on the market. Yet the pleasurable pursuit of supplies can also be a source of frustration, particularly if you are new to this craft. Visiting a bead shop, looking through a catalog, or shopping on a website makes it immediately clear that there are many decisions to make.

The Materials entries for each project in this book ease this process. You'll learn the wire gauge; size and shape of beads, crystals, and pearls; type and size of findings; recommended metal; link size for chains; and many other details that will help you achieve a look similar to the piece that is featured in the accompanying photograph. The Materials entries do, however, make some assumptions, which follow:

- All wire is round, unless specified otherwise.
- Jump ring measurements are the outer diameter.
- Charm measurements are length only.
- Beads, crystals, and pearls are length-drilled unless specified otherwise.
- A charm already has a loop attached at the top; beads, stones, or any other object not called a charm in the materials list will need to be wrapped or threaded in order to attach to a bracelet or necklace chain, or ear wire.

Keep in mind that you might not be able to find an exact match for a vintage chain, finding, or piece of jewelry. In these situations, trust your sense of design and color, as well as your taste, to find a substitution. The same approach can also be applied to any of the beads.

Attaching Charms

Position loops and jump rings so that dangles (bead stacks on head pin, or charms) will face front when attached to the chain.

On a link chain bracelet, this means that the dangles should be attached to the lower portion of a link, or to the front of link (figure 1).

fig. 1

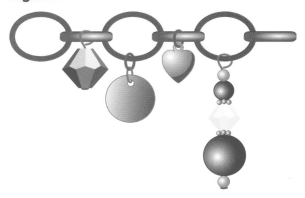

As you connect your charms, the chain can twist. To ensure that the charms face the same direction, reposition the bracelet after you connect each charm.

Designer's Tip

You can change the size of the loop by positioning the wire deeper inside the pliers, where the barrels are wider.

Using Jump Rings

You will find that all jump rings have been cut through somewhere on the perimeter. You use this opening to thread on beads, head pin loops, and other jewelry items. There is a specific technique for opening and closing a jump ring so that the shape is not distorted.

Using two pairs of pliers, grasp each end of the jump ring at the cut (photo 1). Open the jump ring by pulling one side toward you and the other side away from you. If your supplies are limited, use chain-nose pliers and round-nose pliers for this process. The ideal is to use two sets of chain-nose pliers, because round-nose pliers tend to slip. Never pull the ends apart. To close a jump ring, simply reverse the process by twisting the ends back together.

photo 1

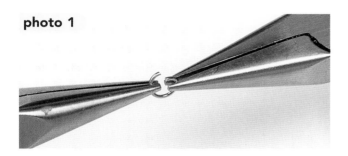

Rolling Simple Loops

A simple loop can be made at the top of a head pin, or at the end of a piece of wire. As you make your first loop, keep in mind that you want it to be round and centered above the beads or charm that are underneath.

1. Thread the desired beads. Above the uppermost item, bend the wire to a 90° angle. Cut off the wire to ⅜-inch (.95 cm) long. Some designers recommend a ¼-inch (.6 cm) length.

2. Grasp the end of the wire in your round-nose pliers (photo 2). Roll the wire around the closed barrels of the pliers until the end of the wire touches the bend (photo 3). Remove the pliers.

photo 2   **photo 3**

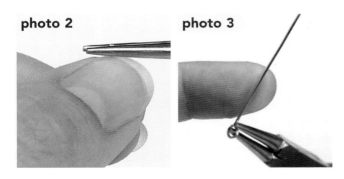

Making Wrapped Loops

Wrapped loops are more durable than simple loops because they are permanent. You do not have to worry about them opening accidentally. The drawback to wrapped loops is that you need to plan the position of your dangles carefully if you want to attach the dangles by the loop in the head pin. (The solution to this disadvantage is to attach dangles by inserting a jump ring through the finished wrapped loop. The jump ring can then be closed around the chain link.)

Here is the process for making a wrapped loop.

1. Use your chain-nose pliers to grasp the wire directly above the last item that you threaded onto it. Bend the wire to a 90° angle (figure 2). Set aside the chain-nose pliers.

2. Grasp the bend in the wire with your round-nose pliers. Wrap the wire around the barrel of the pliers to form half a loop. Reposition the pliers and then complete the rest of the loop (figure 3). Remove the round-nose pliers.

fig. 2   **fig. 3**

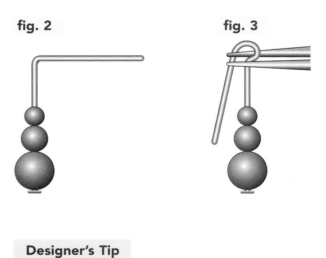

Designer's Tip

After you snip off a piece of wire or the top of a head pin, take the time to smooth the edge with sandpaper. This will protect delicate skin from damage when you are wearing the piece.

3. With the chain-nose pliers, open the loop just enough to slip it onto the chain link. Close the loop.

4. Wrap the end of the wire around the stem until the wraps reach the top of the bead stack (figures 4 and 5). Cut off the excess wire.

fig. 4

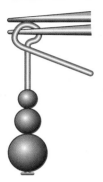

fig. 5

Designer's Tip

You can finish off the tip of the cut wire so the finished piece does not scratch your skin by tucking the end underneath the last wrap. Some designers also squeeze the wrap, which secures the end and also tightens the wraps.

Making Triangular Wraps

Experienced jewelers will recognize this as the wrap they make for a briolette (a tip-drilled oval, pear, or teardrop bead). This same wrap also looks great on a bead that is drilled through the width, or a bicone you want to position horizontally.

1. Cut a piece of wire 2-inches (5 cm) long. With the flat-nose pliers, bend up the last ½ inch (1.3 cm) of the wire. Thread a bead onto the wire.

2. Fold up the other side of the wire until the pieces cross directly above the bead, creating a hat (figure 6).

3. Take the chain-nose pliers to the base of the longer wire, and bend it back down a bit. Use the round-nose pliers to make a simple loop (figure 7).

fig. 6

fig. 7

4. Finish the piece by wrapping the end of the longer wire around the base several times. Snip off the excess wire and file the end, or else tuck it underneath the last loop.

Reaming Beads

When the hole in a bead is too small to fit onto a wire, head pin, or finding you can make it larger. It is not worth the effort to ream a seed bead, or any other inexpensive bead. Semiprecious stones or artisan beads, on the other hand, are ideal candidates for this process.

You can use a manual or electric bead reamer.

1. Stick the bead to a small piece of poster putty.

2. Begin reaming. Tips are diamond-coated, so using the reamer dry too often will wear off this surface. Instead, try to keep the tip wet. If using a manual tool, you can work with the reamer submerged in a shallow bowl of water or held under running water. Never do this with an electric reamer. Instead, dip the drill bit in a small cup of water whenever it feels like the bead is sticking. Stop when you are midway through the bead's hole. Work slowly for maximum control, and do not push too hard.

3. Remove the putty, flip the bead over and stick the putty on the opposite side. Finish reaming the hole from the newly exposed opening.

Do not ream crystals. They shatter easily. Instead, choose a jump ring or wire to fit the hole. The jump ring size that fits in the crystal's hole will be sufficient to support the crystal, and will be strong enough to last with regular, everyday wear.

Drilling Holes in Metal

Whether you are making a hole to string an item or make a rivet, the process is basically the same. You can use a flex shaft or an electric, handheld rotary tool. While drilling a hole may take a few moments longer using a manual drill, you have more control.

1. Mark the hole position with a fine-tip permanent pen. (Some jewelers skip this step.) Do not mark the hole position too close to an edge, particularly when working with soft metal such as sterling silver, which can tear when drilled.

2. Place the charm or piece of metal on an anvil. Create a divot at the marked spot. You can do this by positioning the tip of an awl or a center punch at the hole mark, and then tapping the top with a hammer (figure 8).

fig. 8

3. You may want to clamp the item to a piece of wood, to prevent the metal piece from spinning while drilling. Position the tip of the drill bit in the divot and begin drilling. Do not force the drill bit through the metal. Drill slow and steady, letting the drill do the work.

For a thicker item, you might want to start with a drill bit that makes a hole smaller than you need. After creating the first hole, you can enlarge it with a drill bit that is for a hole the desired finished size.

4. After drilling, smooth the rough edges with a file, and then sandpaper.

Using Crimp Beads and Tubes

Crimping creates a loop with beading wire for attaching a clasp, but you can adapt crimps for other uses.

The process starts with either a crimp tube or bead. As you do more crimping, you will find that you prefer one shape over another.

1. Slide the crimp bead or tube onto the beading wire.

2. Turn the wire and insert it back through the crimp bead or tube, starting at the same end from which it just emerged. Leave a small loop of beading wire.

3. Place the crimp bead or tube in the crimp tool and close it (figure 9). When the crimp bead or tool curls slightly, remove it from the crimp tool.

fig. 9

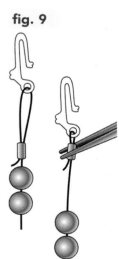

4. Cut the end of the wire at the bottom of the crimp bead or tube. If desired, you can cut it long enough to thread through the closest few beads on the strand.

5. If desired, place the crimp cover around the crimp bead or tube. Grasp the cover with the end of the crimp tool and gently squeeze to secure it.

Tying Knots

You only need to know a few knots to create the pieces that are featured in this book.

Half Hitch Knot

Also known as a simple knot, you make this on a strand of beading cord or thread, next to a bead.

1. Form a loop in the cord, and pass the cord end through the loop (figure 10).

2. Insert the tweezers through the loop and grasp the working cord next to the last bead. Pull the cord gently to slide the loop along the cord until it is next to the bead (figure 11). Pull the knot tightly.

fig. 10   **fig. 11**

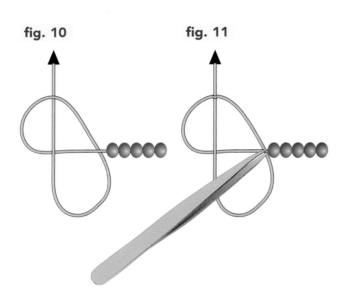

The standard length for necklaces are as follows:
Choker: 15 to 16 inches (38. 1 to 40.6 cm)
Princess: 18 inches (45.7 cm)
Matinee: 20 to 26 inches (50.8 to 66 cm)
Opera: 28 to 36 inches (71.1 to 91.4 cm)
Lariate or rope: 48 inches (121.9 cm)

Overhand Knot

You might know this as a granny knot.

1. Form a loop in the cord or thread.

2. Pull the end of the cord that is underneath, through the loop and pull both ends to tighten the knot (figure 12).

fig. 12

Double Knot

This is very similar to an overhand knot.

1. Form a loop in the cord or thread.

2. Bring one end of the cord or thread through the loop, to go over and under the loop. At this point, you have an overhand knot.

3. Do not tighten the knot. Instead, continue by wrapping the same end of the cord or thread over and under the loop a second time.

Personalizing Fit

Do you have slim—or strong—wrists? You might want to tweak the length of your bracelets so that they look just right on your body.

1. Measure your wrist, and allow a bit of slack for a comfortable fit.

2. Subtract the length of the clasp. This gives you the length of chain that you need.

FLOWER POWER

Roll some loops, stitch a few seed beads, attach some dangles, and you're ready to channel some vibrant energy.

Materials

Designer: Candie Cooper

Finished size: To fit the purchased bracelet

4 turquoise plastic flower spacer beads, 10 mm

6 orange plastic flower spacer beads, 10 mm

16 multicolor 8° seed beads

2 white felt balls with beads, 12 mm

2 red flower spacer beads, 12 mm

2 turquoise swirl glass beads, 8 mm

Orange polka-dot bead, 12 mm

2 brass bird charms, 12 mm

4 green glass leaf charms, 13 mm

5 bright color felt flowers, ¾ inch (1.9 cm) thick

4 silver plated jump rings, 6 mm

4 silver plated jump rings, 5 mm

5 silver plated head pins, 2 inches (5 cm) long

3 silver plated eye pins, 2 inches (5 cm) long

6-inch (15.2 cm) length of 18-gauge silver plated wire

Silver plated 9 mm bracelet with clasp

Craft glue

Sewing thread to match felt flowers

(Continued on next page)

Instructions

1. Glue one turquoise plastic flower bead to the center of each side of the blue felt flower. Attach turquoise and orange plastic flower beads to both sides of the remaining felt flowers.

2. With thread on the hand-sewing needle, anchor the end with a few stitches through the center of one of the felt flowers. String one seed bead onto the needle. Pull the needle and thread down through the center of a plastic flower and out through the opposite side (bottom) of the felt flower. String another seed bead onto the needle, and pull the needle and thread back through the center of the felt flower. Don't pull through the plastic flower and bead on top. Make several small stitches in the middle of the flower center and then trim off the thread ends. Repeat this step for the remaining felt flowers.

3. Cut the tip of one of the head pins at an angle and poke it through the felt flower (figure 1). Roll a simple loop at the top of the head pin using the round-nose pliers. Complete all of the felt flower charms in the same manner.

fig. 1

4. Attach a bird charm to the loop of an eye pin. Cut the tip of the eye pin at an angle. String one seed bead, felt ball, and seed bead onto the pin. Finish the end of the wire with a simple loop, taking care not to squish the ball when you bend the eye pin. Make another bird dangle in the same way.

Tools

Chain-nose pliers, 2 pair

Flat-nose pliers

Round-nose pliers

Wire cutters

Hand-sewing needle

Scissors

Techniques

Using Jump Rings (page 2)

Rolling Simple Loops (page 3)

5. Make a loop at one end of the wire. String a red flower spacer bead onto the wire, followed by a clear and turquoise swirl glass bead and finish it with a simple loop (figure 2). Position the two loops perpendicular to each other by grasping one loop with the flat-nose pliers and the other with the chain-nose pliers and twisting them into place. Repeat this step to make a second flower link.

fig. 2

6. Remove the clasp from the bracelet. Add the length of the chain plus the lengths of the two flower links and the clasp. Compare this to the length you want your bracelet to be, and remove chain links, if necessary (see Personalizing Fit, page 6). Open the loop at the bottom of the flower bead link and connect it to one end of the chain. Attach the remaining flower link to the opposite end of the chain. Connect the clasp to a remaining loop on either of the flower bead links.

7. String a seed bead, the polka-dot bead, and a seed bead onto an eye pin, and finish the pin with a simple loop. Use the bottom loop to connect a felt flower charm. Use the top loop to connect the dangle to the center link of the bracelet.

8. Spread the bracelet horizontally in front of you. Lay the remaining charms out so they are evenly spaced. Attach them along the chain, using 6 mm jump rings for the leaf charms, and 5 mm jump rings for the flower charms. Attach the felt ball dangles with the loop at the top.

9

Sparkling gems in varying shapes
tumble from simple ear wires.

Instructions

Make two.

1. Cut the silver chain into five sections, varying the lengths from ¾ to 1½ inches (1.9 to 3.8 cm).

2. Place a faceted stone, face down, on a flat surface. Place the setting, also face down, on top of the stone. Press down on the setting until you feel the stone click into it. Check to ensure that the stone is seated properly and adjust it, if necessary. If the stone isn't seated properly the first time, you can try to adjust using a toothpick or remove it and try again. If the prongs don't seem to want to let the stone in, you could use the chain-nose pliers to adjust one prong open to allow the stone to be gripped in place. However, the settings are calibrated and typically are ready for setting!

3. Using the chain-nose pliers, gently squeeze the prongs on both sides of the stone, to only slightly move them (figure 1), working your way around the setting until the stone is secure and all of the prongs are against the stone.

fig. 1

4. Cut a 3-inch (7.6 cm) length of wire. Place your round-nose pliers in the center of the cut length of wire. Begin a wrapped loop but, before wrapping, slip the top of the setting onto the wire. Continue with the wrapped loop, capturing the setting inside it (figure 2). Make another wrapped loop with the remaining section of wire, capturing the last link of one length of chain. Seat the remaining stones in their settings and secure a wrapped loop wire to each one, while attaching a length of chain.

fig. 2

5. Slip the ends of the chains for three stones onto a small jump ring, and close it. Slip two lengths of chain—without stones attached—onto another small jump ring, and close it. Attach a large jump ring to the charm, and close it. Slip the jump rings for the charm and the chain onto another large jump ring, and close it. Slip the lower loop of one ear wire and the jump rings for the dangles onto another large jump ring, and close it.

Designer: Tamara Honaman

Finished size: 4 inches (10.2 cm)

Materials

Citrine oval, 8 mm

Trillion amethyst triangular, 8 mm

Pear peacock topaz, 8 mm

2 coin charms, 20 mm

Oval stone setting, 8 mm

Pear stone setting, 8 mm

Triangular stone setting, 8 mm

6 sterling silver jump rings, 5 mm

4 sterling silver jump rings, 4 mm

2 sterling silver French ear wires with bead

18-inch (45.7 cm) length of 24-gauge sterling silver wire

10-inch (25.4 cm) length of 1.5 mm fine sterling silver rolo chain

Tools

Chain-nose pliers, 2 pair

Round-nose pliers

Wire cutters

Techniques

Making Wrapped Loops (page 3)

Designer's Tips

You know a stone is seated properly in a setting when you can look across the surface of the stone and it reflects the light on an even plane and, if you run your finger across the surface, the stone does not budge.

The set stones are attached to the chain with a double-wrapped loop. This requires more wire than a basic wire-wrap because one loop captures the setting and another connects to a link in the chain.

FACES

Keep loved ones close at hand with charms that are a snap to make.

Designer: Jean Campbell

Finished size: 7 inches (17.8 cm)

Materials

14 flat, smooth-face brass buttons with shanks, 7/16 to 5/8 inch (1.1 to 1.6 cm)

10 decorative buttons with shanks, 7/16 to 5/8 inch (1.1 to 1.6 cm)

Red, smoke, and white accent beads: glass pyramid, potato pearl, twisted hex, seed, bicone crystal, and druk, 3 to 6 mm

Sterling silver head pins, 2 inches (5 cm) long

Brass jump rings, 7 mm

2 brass jump rings, 5 mm

7-inch (17.8 cm) length of 8 mm heavy cable brass chain

Brass lobster clasp

14 small black-and-white photographs

Craft glue

Clear-coat acrylic sealer

Tools

Chain-nose pliers, 2 pair

Round-nose pliers

Pencil

Scissors

Craft mini-iron

Techniques

Using Jump Rings (page 2)

Rolling Simple Loops (page 3)

Instructions

1. Match a photograph to one of the buttons for size. Make sure the image you would like captured is smaller than the face of the button. Center and trace a flat, smooth-face button onto the photograph. Cut the photograph inside the traced pencil line.

2. Carefully singe the edges of the photograph with the craft iron. Glue the photograph onto the button. After the glue is dry, cover the mounted photograph with sealer. Attach a 7 mm jump ring to the button's shank. Close the ring. Make 13 more photograph charms in the same manner.

3. Open a 5 mm jump ring and use it to attach one end of the chain to the lobster clasp. Close the ring. Attach the remaining part of the clasp to the opposite end of the chain using the last 5 mm jump ring.

4. Use the jump ring on each photograph charm to attach these items to the chain links at the desired points. Add a jump ring to each of the decorative buttons, and attach them to the chain.

5. String each accent bead onto a head pin. String some head pins with several beads, such as a combination of seed and twisted hex beads, to create larger dangles, finishing each with a wrapped loop. Using a jump ring, attach each of these dangles to the chain.

6. Place each pearl on a head pin, and secure the top with a wrapped loop to make a dangle. String three pearl dangles onto a jump ring and attach the ring to the chain (figure 1). Make and attach additional pearl-cluster dangles.

fig. 1

Designer's Tip

The clasp on this bracelet is intentionally small so it is hidden when the bracelet is worn.

VINTAGE

Challenge traditional ideas about charms with a necklace made from safety pins, vintage chain, and found objects.

Designer: Linda Larsen

Finished size: 24 inches (61 cm)

Materials

9 gray freshwater pearls, 10 mm

13 brass charms, 20 to 30 mm

Vintage metal objects: such as game pieces, keys, locks, bus token, button, and bolt; 12 to 25 mm

36 inches (91.4 cm) brass 18-gauge wire

13 brass safety pins, 1 inch (2.5 cm) long

2 brass safety pins, 1½ inches (3.8 cm) long

Brass safety pin for most of the found objects

Brass jump rings, as needed for found objects

63-inch (157.5 cm) length of vintage 10 mm brass chain

Antiquing, liver of sulphur, or patina solution

Tools

Chain-nose pliers, 2 pair

Round-nose pliers

Wire cutters

Fine-tip permanent marker

Center punch and hammer

Safety glasses

Drill and ¹⁄₁₆-inch (1.6 mm) drill bit

Techniques

Using Jump Rings (page 2)

Reaming Beads (page 4)

Drilling Holes in Metal (page 5)

Note: You may not be able to find some of the exact charms shown in the featured piece. These are found objects that have caught the designer's eye. Use the descriptions—and look at the photos—for inspiration so that you can track down your own special finds.

Instructions

1. Cut three strands of chain to 19, 21, and 23 inches (48.3, 53.3, 58.4 cm) long.

2. Oxidize or apply the antiquing or patina solution to all of the metal: chain, charms, safety pins, and found objects.

3. Feed the last link of the shortest length of chain onto an open, small safety pin. Attach another small safety pin onto the last link of the longest chain. Join the safety pins to make one long length.

4. Grasp a link 1½ inches (3.8 cm) from one end. Slide this link onto one of the large safety pins. Beyond the small safety pins 1 inch (2.5 cm), slide another link onto the remaining large safety pin. Use a small safety pin to attach the loose end of the chain to the first large safety pin (figure 1).

fig. 1

Designer's Tip

You can use a butane or propane torch to darken metal. Place the piece on a fire brick and slowly pass the flame back and forth until you like the color change. You can also bake metal in a toaster oven. After applying a solution to age a metal piece, you can spray a matte sealer to stabilize the finish. This also prevents a finish from rubbing off on clothing.

5. Grasp a link 2 inches (5 cm) from the end of the remaining, 21-inch (53.3 cm) length of chain. Slide this onto the first large safety pin. Slide the last link of the opposite end of this chain onto a small safety pin. Feed this small safety pin through the other large safety pin and close them. Join the two large safety pins, end to end. This will be the clasp.

6. Thread each pearl onto a small safety pin. Use the safety pins to attach the pearls along the chains. Pearls may have to be reamed to fit on the safety pins. If necessary, bend the pins to close around the pearls.

7. Add the charms and found objects randomly along the chains, using safety pins to attach them. If you have something that will not lay right with the safety pin connection, use a jump ring instead. Some pieces may look better if attached with an organic wire wrap that is created by making a loop in the wire with your round-nose pliers, attaching the item, and then bringing up the end of the wire to make a loose wire wrap (figure 2).

fig. 2

8. Make a small divot using the center punch and hammer where you want to place a hole in the token and other metal objects that need a hole. With the back of the token facing you and wearing safety glasses, drill the hole.

OUTRAGEOUS

Extravagant…over-the-top…Use the largest crystals and craziest charms you can find to give this eye-catching piece its extreme personality.

OUTRAGEOUS

Designer: Linda Larsen

Finished size: 7 inches (17.8 cm)

Materials

10 sterling silver rondelle spacers, 4 mm

5 faceted round crystals, 18 mm

3 vintage round sterling silver balls with set crystals, 18 mm

5 freshwater pearls (rice), 18 mm

7 sterling silver charms, 25 to 51 mm

10 sterling silver bead caps, 10 mm

22 sterling silver jump rings, 10 mm

Sterling silver toggle clasp

8 ball-end sterling silver head pins, 2½ inches (6.4 cm) long

16-inch (40.6 cm) length of 16-gauge sterling silver wire

6½-inch (16.5 cm) length of 13 mm sterling silver chain

Scraps of 2-mm chain to total 15 inches (38.1 cm)

Tools

Chain-nose pliers, 2 pair

Round-nose pliers

Flush wire cutters

Pencil

Techniques

Using Jump Rings (page 2)

Rolling Simple Loops (page 3)

Making Wrapped Loops (page 3)

Reaming Beads (page 4)

Instructions

1. Connect all of the charms, evenly distributed, to links on the oversize chain, using a jump ring for each one.

2. Slide a rondelle spacer, crystal, and rondelle spacer onto a ball-end head pin. Make a wrapped loop above the upper rondelle spacer. Open a jump ring and slip the loop onto it, attach the crystal on the first link of the oversize chain, and close the jump ring. Assemble and attach the remaining crystal dangles in the same manner, evenly spacing them along the chain.

3. Thread each of the silver balls with set crystals onto a ball-end head pin, and make a simple loop at the top (wrapping the wire twice around the tip of the round-nose pliers). Attach these dangles to the oversize chain using jump rings.

4. Cut three lengths of tiny chain: 1¼, 1, and ¾ inches (3.2, 2.5, and 1.9 cm). Cut a 3-inch (7.6 cm) length of wire. Make a simple loop at one end, using the round-nose pliers. Open it with the chain-nose pliers, add the end link of each piece of small chain, and then close the loop. Add a bead cap, a freshwater pearl, and another bead cap to the wire. Finish the top of the dangle with a wrapped loop. (You may have to ream out the pearl to get the wire through.) Make four more pearl dangles in the same manner.

5. Attach all of the pearl dangles to the oversize chain with jump rings, as shown in figure 1.

fig. 1

6. Attach the parts of the toggle clasp to the ends of the oversize chain, using jump rings.

TRINKETS

Every child lusts for these plastic geegaws at one time or another. Celebrate your inner child by fashioning them into a pair of amusing ear bobs.

Designer: Terry Taylor

Finished size: Elephants or whistle and ball drops, 1½ inches (3.8 cm); leaf dangles, 3 inches (7.6 cm)

Materials

4 plastic charms, 19 mm

10 matching plastic charms, 19 mm

12 sterling silver jump rings, 6 mm

4 gold-filled French ear wires with bead

2 sterling silver ear studs (ball with drop), 6 mm

2½-inch (6.4 cm) length of 1.5 mm sterling silver chain

Tools

Chain-nose pliers, 2 pair

Round-nose pliers

Wire cutters

Techniques

Using Jump Rings (page 2)

Instructions

Instructions for Drops

Make two for each set.

1. Open the loop at the bottom of the ear wires.

2. Slide a charm onto each loop, and then securely close the loops (figure 1).

fig. 1

Instructions for Dangles

Make two.

1. Cut the chain in half. Set one piece aside for the second earring.

2. Open all of the jump rings, and slide a charm onto each one. Slip the last link of the chain onto one of the jump rings, and close it. Attach four more charms with jump rings, evenly spaced, along the length of the chain. Place the uppermost charm just a link or two from the top of the chain.

3. Slip another jump ring onto the top link of the embellished chain, and then through the loop at the bottom of the ear stud (figure 2).

fig. 2

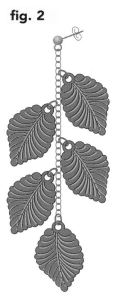

PARIS

A chain brought back from the City of Light was the inspiration for this bracelet. To enhance the memory, charms nestle among crystals salvaged from an old chandelier.

Instructions

Designer: Carol McGoogan

Finished size: 7½ inches (19 cm)

Materials

6 chandelier crystals (top- and bottom-drilled),17 mm

6 silver-filled star charms, 5 mm

3 photo frame charms, 18 mm

22 Paris-theme charms: gold, brass, nickel, copper, and silver-filled, 6 to 13 mm

24 brass jump rings, 4 mm

12 brass head pins (optional, see step 1), 2 inches (5 cm) long

Toggle clasp

7-inch (17.8 cm) length of 4 to 6 mm antiqued brass chain

3 photos or pictures, to fit the frame charms

Clear craft lacquer

Clear drying all-purpose glue stick

Tools

Chain-nose pliers, 2 pair

Flat-nose pliers

Round-nose pliers

Wire cutters

Scissors

Paintbrush (if the lacquer does not include an applicator)

Techniques

Using Jump Rings (page 2)

Rolling Simple Loops (page 3)

Note: You may not be able to find some of the exact charms shown in the featured piece. These are found objects that have caught the designer's eye. Use the descriptions—and look at the photo—for inspiration so that you can track down your own special finds.

1. Spread the chain in front of you, and place the crystals, evenly spaced, along the length of the chain. To attach these, use the wire that connected each crystal to the chandelier. These wire pieces are ideal because each one already has a nice brad on the end. If you do not have the original wire (or are using new crystals), use head pins instead. Insert the wire or head pin, from front to back, through the top hole in the crystal. Trim the wire so it is just long enough to roll a loop over the end of the round-nose pliers. Once the simple loop is formed, the crystal can be attached to the chain using a jump ring.

2. Attach a miniature star to the hole in the bottom of each crystal, again using the original chandelier wire or a head pin (figure 1).

fig. 1

3. Cut a photo or image to fit inside each of the frame charms. Using the glue stick, attach the image to the frame. Cover the image with clear craft lacquer, letting the lacquer seep over the edges of the image and onto the metal surface.

4. Use jump rings to attach the charms to all of the links between the crystals.

5. Use a jump ring at each end of the chain to attach the parts of the toggle clasp.

Designer's Tips

Remove links from the leftover bracelet chain to make perfectly matched jump rings.

Do not shake the bottle of clear craft lacquer, as this will create bubbles you will not be able to remove when you coat your photos. Also, always let this lacquer dry completely, preferably overnight, before handling the piece.

You can never have too many charms!

SOUTHWEST

Sterling silver icons of the Southwest are interspersed with pieces of turquoise and arranged on a basic chain necklace.

Designer: Marlynn McNutt

Finished size: 18 inches (45.7 cm)

Materials

Turquoise nugget, 18 to 22 mm

Turquoise lentil, 10 mm

Sterling silver Kokopelli charm, 30 mm

Sterling silver axe charm, 33 mm

2 sterling silver Zuni bear beads, 13 mm

2 sterling silver feather charms, 31 mm

6 sterling silver jump rings, 6.5 mm

4 sterling silver head pins, 1½ inches
  (3.8 cm) long

Sterling silver lizard toggle clasp

18-inch length of 6 mm sterling silver
  ribbed flat cable chain

Tools

Chain-nose pliers, 2 pair

Round-nose pliers

Flush wire cutters

Techniques

Using Jump Rings (page 2)

Rolling Simple Loops (page 3)

Instructions

1. Open a jump ring, and slip it through the loop in the Kokopelli charm. Find the center link of the chain and close the jump ring around it, to attach the charm.

2. Using another jump ring, add the axe charm to the right of the Kokopelli charm.

3. Run a head pin up through one of the Zuni bears, and finish it with a simple loop. Twist open the loop you just made, thread it through one of the links to the right of the axe, and then close the loop.

4. Use a head pin and simple loop to make a dangle with the turquoise nugget (figure 1).

fig. 1

5. Thread the remaining Zuni bear and the turquoise lentil onto separate head pins, and the feather charms onto jump rings. Attach these elements to the left of the Kokopelli charm.

6. Using a jump ring, attach part of the toggle clasp to one end of the chain. Use the last jump ring to attach the last part of the toggle clasp to the opposite end of the chain.

Designer's Tip

A bead with a hollow body, such as the Zuni bears, might wobble too much when mounted on the head pin. You can control this by placing a small bead or spacer on the head pin before adding the bead. Make sure that the bead or spacer is small enough to slip up inside the hollow body so it is invisible.

HEART TO HEART

Recycling is taken to a new level when old tin gets a new life as bright heart dangles. Just cut shapes from a sheet, rivet, and attach them to your bracelet chain.

Designer: Beth Taylor

Finished size: 7 inches (17.8 cm)

Materials

11 brass or zinc mini eyelets, ³⁄₃₂ inch (2.3 mm)

22 miniature 0-80 brass and silver-plated, hex or fillister head, bolts, ¼ inch (6 mm) long

22 size 0-80 brass and silver-plated washers

13 brass jump rings, 8 mm

Brass toggle clasp

6½-inch (16.5 cm) length of 8-mm brass rolo chain

Sheet of tracing paper

Step 1 Templates 1, 2, and 3

2 self-adhesive name badges

8 x 4-inch (20.3 x 10.2) sheet of tin

Clear acrylic spray-on sealer

(Continued on page 28)

Designer's Tip

Avoid tin from soda and beer cans. It is too thin. Tin for your charms should be at least 27 gauge (.36 mm thick).

Instructions

1. Use the tracing paper to copy the heart templates onto the name badges You need five of template 1, four of template 2, and two of template 3. Cut out the shapes with excess paper around each one. Peel off the backing, and affix the shapes to the plain side of the tin. Cut out the tin shapes, keeping the double hearts attached at the tips.

Template 1   Template 2   Template 3

2. Fold each tin heart in half so the two halves are back-to-back and printed tin is on the outside (figure 1). Hammer lightly with the leather mallet to ensure every folded heart is flat. The edges of the folded halves of each heart may not match. Do not adjust them.

fig. 1

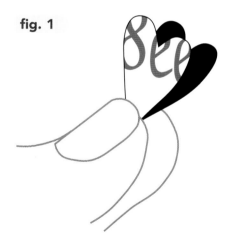

3. With the marker, make a spot for an eyelet at the upper left on one side of each heart. Punch a hole as marked using the two-hole metal punch.

4. Insert an eyelet into the hole made in one heart and lay it, facedown, on the anvil. Insert the eyelet setter into the back of the eyelet (figure 2). Holding the eyelet setter with one hand, squarely hit the top of the eyelet setter with the hammer or leather mallet. The eyelet back should curl down, and the eyelet should be tight and secure, through both layers. Set an eyelet in every remaining heart. On each heart, use the center punch and leather mallet to make divots in the upper right and slightly above the point.

fig. 2

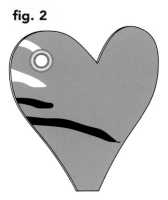

5. Place a heart on top of a piece of scrap wood, and hold it with a small clamp (figure 3). Wearing safety glasses, drill holes at each indentation, through both layers. Drill holes in all of the hearts.

fig. 3

6. Thread a washer onto a bolt. Insert the bolt into one of the holes in a heart, through both layers. Snip off the excess bolt, leaving only a tiny amount exposed above the tin (figure 4). File the end of the bolt so the end is flat. Tap around the edges of the bolt with the riveting hammer. The bolt end will flare out and then end up flush against the tin, forming a tight join.

7. Once each heart has been riveted, file the edges until they are smooth and the layers match. File away from you, in one direction only. Finish by lightly sanding.

8. Evenly spray each side with two to three coats of the clear acrylic sealer.

9. Use jump rings to attach each heart to links along the bracelet chain, and to attach the toggle clasp to the ends.

fig. 4

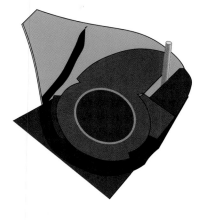

TRUE LOVE

A necklace with potential gets a facelift with a bit of deconstruction—and then reconstruction—using vintage or new chains, dangles, and charms.

Designer: Erikia Ghumm

Finished size: 16 inches (40.6 cm)

Materials

Word bead, 18 mm

Blue glass bead (round), 11 mm

Pink faux pearl (round) 18 mm

Citrine drop, 13 mm

Pearl (round), 6 mm

Rhinestone spacer, 4 mm

Gray freshwater pearl (round), 3 mm

Crystal drop, 8 mm

Faux pearl charm, 5 mm

Glass heart charm, 9 mm

Glass heart charm, 22 mm

Key charm, 20 mm

Watch face charm, 25 mm

3 sterling silver jump rings, 6 mm

Toggle clasp

6 sterling silver bead caps, 6 mm

4 sterling silver head pins, 2 inches
(5 cm) long

Sterling silver ball-end head pin, 2 inches
(5.1 cm) long

5 sterling silver jump rings, 4 mm

7-inch (17.8 cm) length of 16-gauge
sterling silver wire

26-inch-long (66 cm) gold-color chain
necklace with heart locket

11-inch (27.9 cm) length of 8 mm faux
pearl and crystal chain

(Continued on page 32)

Instructions

1. Deconstruct the necklace by cutting off the chain at one side of the locket. On the other side of the necklace, cut off all but 4 inches (10.2 cm) of chain that is closest to the locket.

2. Cut the pearl and crystal chain to three lengths: 1, 4, and 6 inches (2.5, 10.2, and 15.2 cm). Using the larger jump rings, attach part of the clasp to the end of the 4-inch (10.2 cm) length, and attach the remaining part of the clasp to one end of the 6-inch (15.2 cm) length (figure 1).

fig. 1

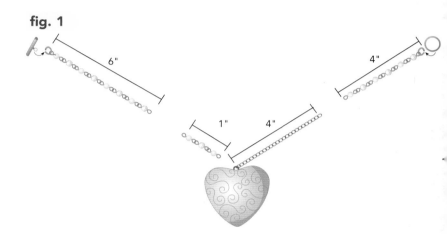

3. Thread the word bead onto the heavy-duty wire. Using the round-nose pliers, make a wrapped loop at both ends of the bead. Do not make this wrap look perfect (see photo below).

Materials (continued)

14-inch (35.6 cm) length of 1 mm curb chain

Piece of plain office paper, slightly larger than the locket

2 photos for the locket

Scrapbooking glue dots

Tools

Chain-nose pliers, 2 pair

Round-nose pliers

Wire cutters

Ruler

Soft-lead pencil

Scissors

Techniques

Using Jump Rings (page 2)

Rolling Simple Loops (page 3)

Making Wrapped Loops (page 3)

4. Thread a bead cap, blue glass bead, and bead cap onto a head pin, and finish with a simple loop. Make two wrapped dangles: On a head pin, thread a bead cap, the large pearl, and a bead cap; on a ball-end head pin thread a bead cap, the citrine, and a bead cap.

5. Slide the small round pearl, spacer, and small gray pearl onto a head pin, and finish it with a simple loop. Use a small jump ring to attach the faux pearl charm to the necklace.

6. Place the paper over the inside of the open locket, and rub over the paper with a pencil to transfer the locket shape. Remove the paper, trim out the shape from the inside, and remove the excess paper to make an opening. Place the opening over the photo, and trace the shape onto the photo. Cut out the shape. Cut a second photo in the same manner. Glue the photos into the locket.

7. Using the two pairs of chain-nose pliers and a jump ring, attach the available end of the 4-inch faux pearl and crystal chain to the loose end of the chain that is still attached to the locket.

8 Open the last link at the available end of the longest piece of pearl and crystal chain. Attach the word bead. At the other end of the word bead, attach the shortest piece of faux pearl and crystal chain. Attach the locket to the other end of this short piece, using a large jump ring.

9. Add the charms and bead dangles to the locket's chain with jump rings.

10. Attach a jump ring to the loop on the citrine dangle, and slide this onto the 14-inch (35.6 cm) length of chain. Add a jump ring to each end of the chain, and use these to attach the ends of the chain to the toggle clasp pieces.

DIVINE

Showcase exquisite padparadschas (the rarest naturally occurring colored crystal) and beautiful polygon crystals in these sweet earrings.

Instructions

Make two Angels and two Crystal Bows.

1. For an Angel earring, thread a polygon crystal, angel wings, pearl, rondelle, and bicone onto a head pin (figure 1). For a crystal bow earring, thread a cube onto a head pin.

2. Finish the dangle with a wrapped head pin. Use the crimp tool to tuck in any excess wire, taking care not to crush the top bead.

3. This step is only for the crystal bow earring. Cut the wire into two 4-inch (10.2 cm) lengths. Set one piece of wire aside to make the matching earring. Position the round-nose pliers 1½ inches (3.8 cm) from the top of the remaining piece of wire. Holding the wire below the pliers, bend the wire away from you to make a right angle. Pull the wire over the top of the nose of the pliers. Remove the pliers. Thread the wire-wrapped cube onto the loop. Holding the open loop tightly with the round-nose pliers, wrap the short end of the wire around the long end three times. Trim off the excess wire on the short end only. Thread the bow and round crystal onto the wire (figure 2). Make a wrapped loop above the crystal.

4. Carefully open the loop on the ear wire, slip on the dangle, and close the ear wire loop.

fig. 1

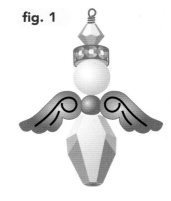

fig. 2

Designer: Bonnie Clewans

Finished sizes: Angel earrings, 1¾ inches (4.4 cm); Crystal Bow earrings 1⅝ inches (4.1 cm)

Angel Materials

2 crystals (polygon), 12 mm

2 pearls (round), 6 mm

2 rhinestone rondelles, 5 mm

2 bicone crystals, 3 mm

2 gold plated pewter angel wings, 8 mm

2 gold filled head pins, 2 inches (5 cm) long

2 lever back ear wires

Crystal Bow Materials

2 padparadscha crystals (cube), 8 mm

2 faceted crystals (round), 3 mm

2 silver plated pewter bows, 10 mm

2 sterling silver head pins, 2 inches (5 cm) long

2 lever back, gold filled ear wires

8-inch (20.3 cm) length of 24-gauge half-hard sterling silver wire

Tools

Round-nose pliers

Fine wire cutters

Crimp tool

Ruler

Glue

Techniques

Making Wrapped Loops (page 3)

Designer's Tip

You can paint the angel wings with nail polish or enamel model paint if you want to add more interest.

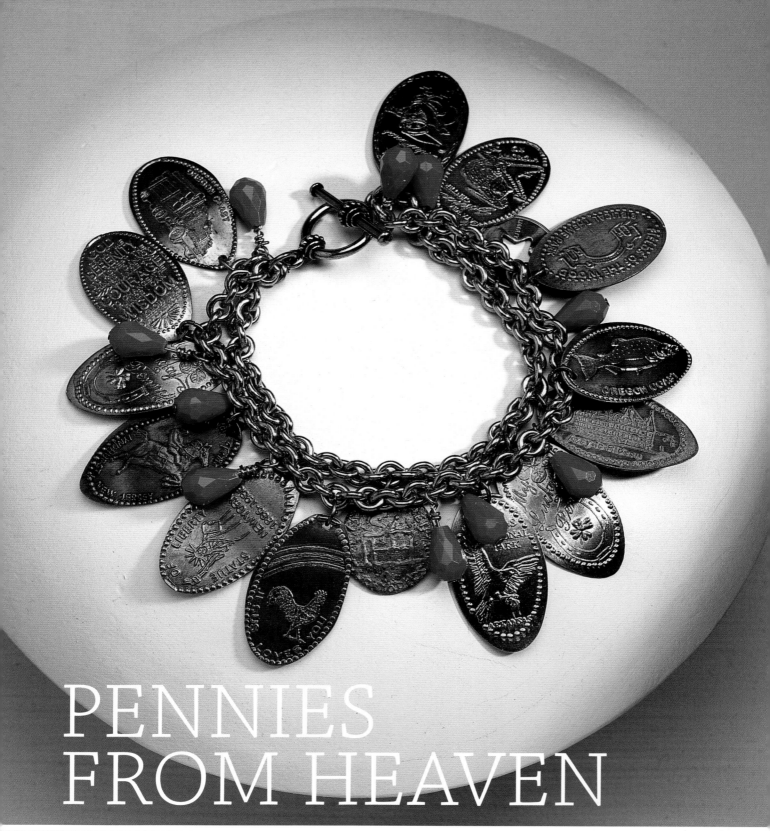

PENNIES FROM HEAVEN

The designer of this bracelet searches for souvenir penny machines everywhere he travels. These charming machines (no pun intended) flatten and imprint a penny with a specially engraved die.

Designer: Terry Taylor

Finished size: 8 inches (20.3 cm)

Materials

10 teardrop beads, 13 mm

15 flat souvenir pennies

10 head pins, 2 inches (5 cm) long

17 copper jump rings, 5 mm

Copper toggle clasp

15-inch (38.1 cm) length of 5 mm copper link chain

1 teaspoon of salt

¼ cup white vinegar

Tools

Chain-nose pliers, 2 pair

Needle-nose pliers

Wire cutters

Rawhide mallet

Shallow glass bowl

Hand towel

Awl or nail with a flat head

Safety glasses

Drill and ⅟₁₆-inch (1.6 mm) drill bit

Half-round file

Techniques

Using Jump Rings (page 2)

Making Wrapped Loops (page 3)

Drilling Holes in Metal (page 5)

Instructions

1. Souvenir pennies may be slightly curved when they come out of the machine. If this is the case, place them on a sturdy work surface, one at a time, and tap on them with a rawhide mallet to flatten them.

2. Pour the salt and vinegar into the bowl. Stir the mix until the salt is dissolved. Place the pennies in the bowl to soak for about 5 minutes. When removed, wipe the pennies with a hand towel to reveal the shiny surface.

3. Use an awl or nail to make a divot at the top of the penny, where you wish to drill a hole (figure 1). Use a small drill bit to create a hole in each penny. Smooth the edges with the file.

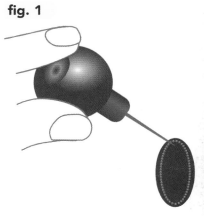

fig. 1

4. Cut the chain into two equal lengths. Spread both pieces in front of you. Plan the finished position of the pennies and beads by placing them underneath the chains. Leave these items in position as you work through the next few steps.

5. Attach pennies to the chain links of both lengths of chain, using a jump ring for each penny.

Designer's Tips

You can purchase flattened pennies online, but that's not as much fun as finding the machine and imprinting your own. You can find them everywhere except in federally owned venues. Why? It's illegal to deface or alter currency for fraudulent purposes. Don't worry, the government won't chase after you when you wear your finished bracelet, because you can't use these pennies in the gum machine, and no cashier will accept them!

If you don't have a rawhide mallet, sandwich a penny between two pieces of scrap wood and flatten the penny with a regular hammer.

6. Slide a bead onto a head pin. Roll the head pin to create a loop. Slide the wire through a chain link (figure 2). Wrap the end of the wire around the head pin that is coming out the top of the bead. Cut off the excess wire. Attach all of the remaining beads to both chain lengths in the same manner.

fig. 2

7. Open a jump ring and slip on part of the toggle clasp and the last link of one end of each chain. Close the jump ring. Use another jump ring to attach the remaining toggle clasp part and the opposite ends of the chains.

GRAMMY'S BAUBLES

Rhinestones! Crystals! Beads! Flowers! This piece has it all. An over-the-top chunky charm bracelet makes the most of vintage earrings and brooches.

GRAMMY'S BAUBLES

Designer: Andrea Trbovich

Finished size: 7 inches (17.8 cm)

Materials

4 sets of vintage earrings, 20 mm

Vintage brooch, 35 mm

6 vintage charms, 5 to 15 mm

15 silver-color jump rings, 10 mm

7-inch (17.8 cm) length of 8 mm silver-color link chain

8-inch (20.3 cm) length of gold-color 10 mm crystal link chain necklace with clasp

Tools

Chain-nose pliers, 2 pair

Flat-nose pliers

Wire cutters

Safety glasses

Drill and .74 to 1.61-mm drill bit

Flat file

Techniques

Using Jump Rings (page 2)

Drilling Holes in Metal (page 5)

Designer's Tip

The metal for the findings, chain, and vintage pieces don't need to match. It is more important that all of the pieces share a theme. For this bracelet, all of the pieces convey the impression of a flower and include at least some blue.

1. Using the wire cutters, carefully remove the earring clips and pin backs from the jewelry pieces. Smooth any rough edges with the file.

2. Pick out the pieces that have filigree, holes, or wiring that you can use to attach a jump ring. Open a jump ring and slip it through a hole—or underneath a secure piece of wire—on an earring or brooch (figures 1 and 2). Twist the jump ring to close it. Add a jump ring to each of the selected pieces and charms in the same manner.

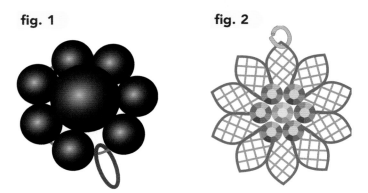

fig. 1   **fig. 2**

3. Gather the remaining jewelry pieces. Drill a hole near the top of each one, through metal only (figure 3). Be cautious you do not shift the arrangement of any beads, crystals, or rhinestones as you drill and wire each piece. If there is not an area that can easily accommodate drilling, choose a position where one small bead or rhinestone could be removed easily without a noticeable loss. Often, a rhinestone will pop out when you start drilling on the back, directly behind the position where the rhinestone is set. File off all of the rough edges, and then insert a jump ring through the hole.

fig. 3

4. Spread the silver-color chain in front of you, and arrange the charms in the manner you would like to attach them. Place the largest piece in the middle. For symmetry, position one piece of each earring set on either side of the center. Use the jump rings to attach the pieces as arranged.

5. Cut the crystal chain to match the bracelet length. Do not cut off the end with the clasp. Open the last link at both ends of the silver-color chain, and close them around the last links of the crystal chain.

FLIGHT OF FANCY

Random bead placement on multiple strands of memory wire lets this piece evolve in unexpected ways.

Instructions

1. Use the all-in-one glue to attach and seal decorative and blue paper to the back and interior of the bezel cup and some of the lockets.

2. Place—do not glue—a charm inside the bezel cup and each locket except the largest one. Close the lockets to make sure they will snap shut with the object inside.

3. Lightly coat the interior bezel cup and lockets with the all-in-one glue to attach the charms and embellish them with fire polish beads, pearls, or semiprecious stones. Pour the clear craft lacquer inside each locket.

Designer: Ndidi Kowalczyk

Finished size: 13 inches (33 cm)

Materials

20 to 50 fire polish beads, pearls, or semiprecious stones, 3 to 8 mm

1 brass focal bead, 20 mm

3 to 4 strands fire-polish faceted beads, 6 mm

1 to 2 strands, each at least 16 inches (40.6 cm) long, of garnet-color tumbled stone chips, 3 to 4 mm

6 dove beads (center drilled), 8 mm

4 crystals, 4 mm

1 strand of filed brass cube beads, 3 mm

Vitrail oval crystal, 24 mm

3 to 4 strands pearls (potato), 8 mm

1 antique brass finish bezel cup with loop 20 mm

Locket, 45 mm

6 lockets, 20 to 25 mm

6 small charms, slightly smaller than each locket (except largest locket)

2 biplane charms, 18 mm

2 brass bead caps to fit the brass focal bead

7 head pins, 2 inches (5 cm) long

14 antique brass finish jump rings, 5 mm

2 split rings, 5 mm

Antique brass finish lobster claw clasp

2 antique brass finish 10-loop end bars

2 cone ends, 6 mm

Stainless steel memory wire necklace with large loops

20-inch (50.8 cm) length of 4 mm base metal cable chain

4-inch (10.2 cm) length of 4 mm base metal cable chain

5-inch (12.7 cm) square of decorative paper

6-inch (15.2 cm) square of blue paper

Water-based, clear-drying all-in-one glue, sealant, and finish

Clear craft lacquer

Tools

Chain-nose pliers, 2 pair

Round-nose pliers

Flush wire cutters

Memory wire shears

Small paintbrush

Small tweezers

Split-ring pliers

Techniques

Using Jump Rings (page 2)

Making Wrapped Loops (page 3)

4. Make a link using the bead caps and the large brass focal bead. Before closing the wrapped loop at the bottom, add a short length of the base metal cable chain. Close the top with a simple loop. Attach the large locket to the bottom of the chain. Create two small dangles to attach along the chain.

5. Make a wrapped loop at the end of a head pin. Cut the head off the head pin. Thread a dove bead and a 4 mm crystal onto the head pin. Make another wrapped loop. Make two more links like this. Use a jump ring to add a locket to the bottom of a dove link. Attach a charm to each of the remaining dove links.

6. Make a wrapped loop dangle on a head pin threaded with a brass cube bead and fire polish bead. Attach this to another link that has only a dove bead.

7. Without cutting off the head on a head pin, make a dangle with a small crystal and dove bead. Using a jump ring, attach 2 links from the base metal chain to the top of the dove bead.

8. Using jump rings, create three dangles by attaching a locket to a ¾-inch (1.9 cm) piece of base metal chain. Make and set aside the following dangles, for use in step 14: Thread a cube and dove bead onto a head pin, and use a simple loop to attach it to the chain on one of the locket dangles. Add a large bead (threaded on a head pin) to another locket dangle. Use a jump ring to add a biplane charm to another locket dangle.

9. Cut a ⅜-inch (9.5 mm) piece of base metal chain. Attach the vitrail oval crystal to one end, using a jump ring.

10. Cut five lengths of memory wire, each with one full rotation plus 3 inches (7.6 cm). Cut three lengths of chain, each 2 inches (5 cm) long, for the spacer bars. Slide an end-link of a spacer bar chain to the center of a length of memory wire.

Designer's Tip

The loops in at least 11 inches (27.9 cm) of the base metal chain must be large enough for the memory wire to feed through. The remaining chain lengths, which are used to join the memory wire loops, can be scrap chain.

11. Add any combination of pearl, cube, stone chip, and fire polish beads to the memory wire, on both sides of the spacer bar chain, ending with a pearl. Continue to string any combination of items until you have covered 1 inch (2.5 cm) of wire on one side of the chain and ¾ inch (1.9 cm) on the other. Slide the top link of the vitrail crystal dangle onto one side and the dove bead dangle on the other.

12. Cover 2 inches (5 cm) on both sides of the chain. Add the next length of spacer bar chain (figure 1). Continue filling the memory wire, for 1 inch (2.5 cm) on both sides.

fig. 1

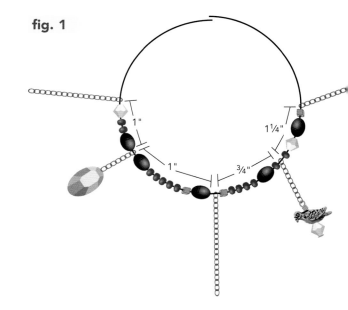

13. Thread another length of the cut memory wire onto the center spacer bar chain, ¼ inch (6 mm) below the link holding the first length of memory wire. String items to cover 2 inches (5 cm) on both sides of the wire (figure 2). Insert the wire through the next length of spacer bar chain. Continue filling the memory wire, randomly adding the dangles you made earlier. Add and cover two more lengths of memory wire in the same manner.

fig. 2

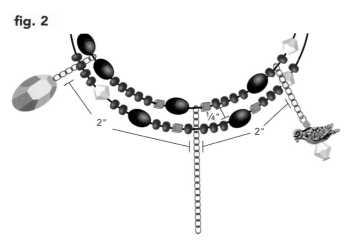

14. Add the last length of memory wire to the central spacer bar chain. String 1 inch (2.5 cm) of pearls and beads to the wire, on each side of the spacer chain. On each side, string one of the dangles that you set aside in step 8. Secure these with several beads and then a pearl. Continue filling the memory wire, randomly adding dangles until just ½ inch (1.3 cm) of the wire remains exposed at the ends.

15. Use the split rings to attach the lobster claw clasp parts to the end bars, adding a biplane charm to one side. Attach the end bars to the necklace, using the round-nose pliers to turn simple loops in the memory wire and connect these to the spacer bar loops. Use the pair of chain-nose pliers to push down on the memory wire loops to close them. Use a 5 mm jump ring to connect a charm or dangle to the last ring of both end bars.

16. Attach the extender chain to one of the split rings. Add a dangle at the bottom of the extender, using a teardrop crystal, head pin, and cone.

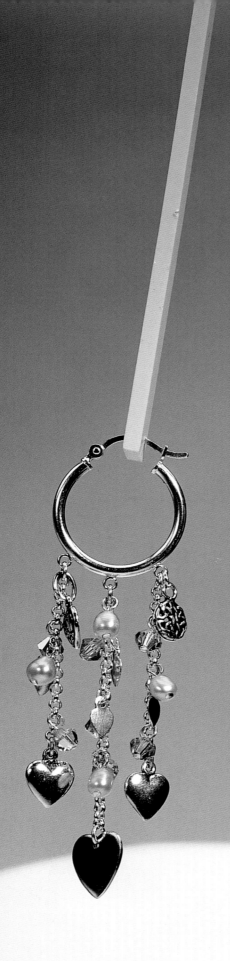

DROPLETS

Delicate charms and crystals command
attention when grouped along dainty chains.

Instructions

Make two.

1. Cut four pieces of chain 1 inch (2.5 cm) long and two pieces of chain 1⅜ inches (3.5 cm) long.

2. Run a head pin through a bicone, and finish with a simple loop. Add a head pin with a simple loop to the remaining bicones and pearls in the same manner.

3. Open the jump rings. Use one to attach each 1-inch (2.5 cm) length of chain to the left outside loop on the ear hoop. In the following steps, use a jump ring to attach each sterling silver charm or drop to a chain link. Attach each bicone and pearl by opening the loop at the top of the head pin.

4. Attach one of the Celtic filigree charms to the left (outside) loop of the ear hoop.

fig. 1

5. From top to bottom along the chain, attach a bicone, pearl, small flat heart, bicone, and small puff heart in the last link (figure 1).

6. Attach a 1-inch (2.5 cm) length of chain to the right (outside) loop of the ear hoop. Also attach a decorative heart to the right loop of the ear hoop. Add the same bicones, charms, drops, and pearls—in the same order and positions—to this chain.

7. Attach the 1⅜-inch (3.5 cm) length of chain to the center loop of the ear hoop. Attach a pearl to this same loop. From top to bottom along this chain, attach a bicone, 3 small flat heart drops, bicone, bicone, pearl, and large heart to the last link (figure 2).

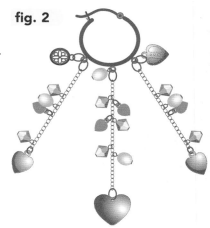
fig. 2

Designer: Marlynn McNutt

Finished size: 2¾ inches (7 cm)

Materials

14 light rose bicone crystals, 4 mm

8 mauve freshwater pearls (potato), 8 mm

2 sterling silver Celtic filigree charms, 6 mm

8 sterling silver flat heart charms, 5 mm

4 sterling silver puff heart charms, 8 mm

2 sterling silver decorative heart charms, 11 mm

2 sterling silver smooth, flat heart drops, 10 mm

22 sterling silver head pins, 2 inches (5 cm) long

2 sterling silver ear hoops with 3 loops, 15 mm

24 sterling silver jump rings, 3 mm

7-inch (17.8 cm) length of 2 mm sterling silver rolo chain

Tools

Chain-nose pliers, 2 pair

Round-nose pliers

Flush wire cutters

Techniques

Rolling Simple Loops (page 3)

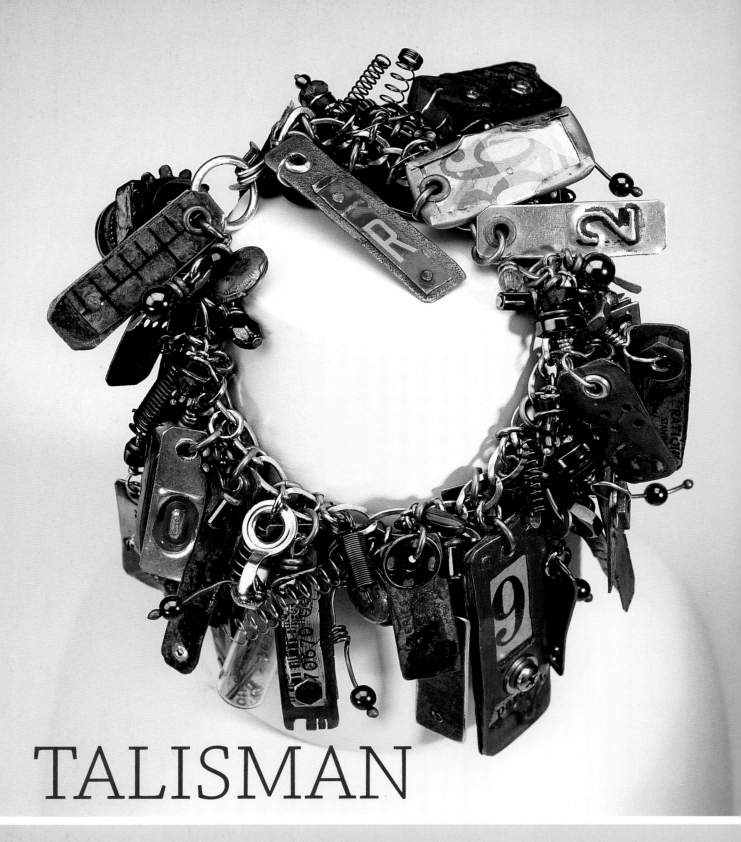

TALISMAN

Repetition of shapes unifies a quirky assortment of metal plates and found objects.

Materials

Designer: Susan Lenart Kazmer

Finished size: 7 inches (17.8 cm)

Materials

Dark-color beads, 5 to 8 mm

Tube of dark-color 11° seed beads

Brass, copper, sterling silver, or stainless steel rectangular found objects, 10 x 25 mm to 9 x 40 mm

Brass, copper, and stainless steel circular found objects, 10 to 30 mm

22-gauge sterling silver sheet metal

Jump rings in various metals, 5 to 8 mm

Ball-end sterling silver head pins, 2 inches (5 cm) long

Sterling silver eye pins, 2 inches (5 cm) long

Sterling silver clasp

24-gauge base metal wire

16-gauge annealed steel wire

6½-inch (16.5 cm) length of 6 mm base metal chain

Antiquing, liver of sulphur, or patina solution

Matte medium

Paper printed with images and words, to fit the found objects

Thin sheet of mica or clear, hard plastic

Note: You may not be able to find some of the exact charms shown in the featured piece. These are found objects that have caught the designer's eye. Use the descriptions—and look at the photos—for inspiration so that you can track down your own special finds.

(Continued on page 50)

Instructions

1. Cut the sheet metal into rectangles ranging from ⅜ to ⅝ inch (9.5 mm to 1.6 cm) wide and 1 to 2 inches (2.5 to 5 cm) long. Cut several pairs to the same size. Use the metal file to clean up and smooth the edges by pushing the file away from you. Oxidize or apply the antiquing or patina solution to the rectangles. Glue very small scraps of paper to some of the pieces with the matte medium. Set aside the matching rectangles for use in step 2.

2. Select two scraps of paper to showcase between two matching pieces of flat metal. Draw a rectangle with a fine-tip permanent marker where you want to cut out a window that will allow you to see the paper inside when the riveting is finished. Drill a hole in a corner of the window. Insert the blade of the jeweler's saw into the hole and fix the other end into the saw. Saw along the drawn lines until the center falls out. Use the metal file to clean up and smooth the edges by pushing the file away from you. Make a matching window in the other piece of metal.

3. Cut two pieces of mica or clear, hard plastic, both slightly larger than the window. Place the mica under each window, with a paper image on top.

4. Stack all the layers (silver sheet metal, mica, paper image [face down], paper image [faceup], mica, and silver sheet metal) with the metal edges aligned (figure 1). Place the stack in a small clamp. Drill straight through all the layers at a corner.

fig. 1

Tools (continued)

Chain-nose pliers, 2 pair

Flat-nose pliers

Round-nose pliers

Flush wire cutters

Metal file

Fine-tip permanent marker

Jeweler's saw and blade

Small clamp

Safety glasses

Drill and 1/16-inch (1.6 mm) drill bit

Anvil

Small ball peen hammer

Small paintbrush

Techniques

Using Jump Rings (page 2)

Rolling Simple Loops (page 3)

Making Wrapped Loops (page 3)

Making Triangular Wraps (page 4)

Designer's Tip

Rivets are the strongest method of attaching metal to metal besides soldering. For a piece that has unusual materials, such as wood, paper, and plastic, you don't have the option of soldering since these materials wouldn't survive the heat.

5. Place the stack on an anvil. Insert the annealed wire, that has been filed, all the way into the hole. This should be a tight fit. Place the flush wire flat against the top sheet. Raise the cutters just less than 3/8 inch (9.5 mm) above the sheet metal, and snip off the wire (figure 2). Do not move the stack. Using a very small ball peen hammer, tap gently around the out side of the extended wire until the top starts to look like a nail head.

fig. 2

6. Gently turn over the stack, and work the other side in the same manner. Once your first rivet is complete, there will be less shifting and you can then drill the rest of the holes. Work all of the holes in the same manner, and file them so they are smooth and clean. Make at least four rivets in a small piece, and then check for buckling. You may need to add another two to four rivets. Complete as many window rectangles as desired.

7. Smaller items could be lost amid the larger pieces. The solution is to combine several small objects as a single dangle. For example, thread a seed bead onto a 2-inch (5 cm) ball-end head pin, and then stack several small metal disks and washers on top. Finish with a simple loop. Combine items on head pins to create dangles.

8. As necessary, drill holes at the top and bottom of items, attach a piece of 24-gauge base metal wire, and then roll a loop for each hole.

9. The effect of this bracelet is created by using mostly long pieces, combining several smaller found objects to create a longer dangle, and by using many pivot points. Make links by combining several pieces on an eye pin, and then rolling a simple loop at the top. Now you can use a jump ring to attach the top of a smaller, metal rectangle to the bottom of the link. Small springs that you find inside some pens make excellent links: Unwind the very top and bottom of the spring, and wrap each of the ends around jump rings (figure 3).

fig. 3

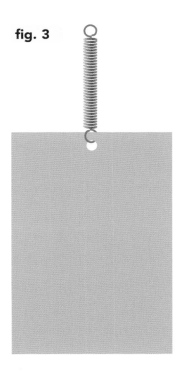

10. Continue building dangles. You need enough to attach at least one dangle on each side of every link in the bracelet chain. As you work, consider using wrapped loops, rather than simple loops, at the top of some dangles. Simple loops are the easiest, but a triangular wrap will allow a drop bead to move. This will add more visual texture to your finished piece.

11. Use jump rings to attach the clasp to the chain, and then attach the dangles to the chain, again using jump rings.

MEMENTOS

Extend earrings to
new lengths with a link
made from another charm.

Instructions

Materials

2 stamps in photo charms, 24 mm

2 sterling silver imitation subway tokens, 18 mm

2 French ear wires with wire wrap and ball

2 sterling silver jump rings, 3.5 mm

Tools

Chain-nose pliers, 2 pair

Flat-nose pliers

Safety glasses

Drill and ¹⁄₁₆-inch (1.6 mm) drill bit

Round needle file

Techniques

Using Jump Rings (page 2)

Drilling Holes in Metal (page 5)

1. Make a divot at the top and bottom of the subway token by making a quick twist with the tip of the drill bit at the desired spots. Silver is soft enough to indent easily. Place the bit in the drill, and make a hole at each divot. File the rough edges around the holes.

2. Use the two chain-nose pliers to grip the sides of a jump ring. Twist the sides apart to open it. Thread the stamp charm and bottom hole of the subway token charm onto the jump ring (figure 1). Close the ring securely.

fig. 1

3. Using flat-nose pliers, twist open the loop at the bottom of the ear wire. Thread the top of the subway token onto the open loop. Twist the loop to close it.

Designer's Tip

Be sure to stay well within the border on the subway token when drilling. If the hole is too close to the edge, it will compromise the structural integrity of the charm.

SPRINGTIME

Rejuvenate vintage jewelry with crystals and glass beads.

Instructions

Designer: Candie Cooper

Finished size: Bird 3 inches (7.6 cm);
    flower, 3 inches (7.6 cm)

Swallow Materials

3 blue glass beads, 6 mm

Brass nest charm, 25 mm

Brass treble clef charm, 12 mm

Music note charm, 8 mm

Bird brooch, 2 inches (5 cm)

6 brass bead caps, 5 mm

4 gold-color jump rings, 5 mm

3 gold-color eye pins, 2 inches (5 cm) long

Tie tack

1-inch (2.5 cm) length of 4 mm old
    brass chain

Craft glue with precision applicator

Flower Materials

2 AB crystal beads (round), 8 mm

Pink glass pearl bead (round), 6 mm

Brass leaf charm, 15 mm

2 brass bell bead caps to fit the crystals

2 brass bead caps, 5 mm

Flower brooch, 1¼ inches (3.2 cm)

2 gold-color jump rings, 5 mm

2 gold-color head pins, 2 inches (5 cm) long

1 gold-color eye pin, 2 inches (5 cm) long

(Continued on page 56)

Swallow Instructions

1. Scratch up the flat back of the tie tack finding by rubbing it with the coarse sandpaper. Place a dot of glue on the back of the nest charm, and push the flat side of the tie tack into the glue. Make sure that some of the adhesive comes up around the edge of the finding.

2. String a bead cap, blue bead, and bead cap onto an eye pin, and roll a simple loop at the top, using the tip of the round-nose pliers. Make two more dangles in the same manner. Remove one link from the chain, and use it to connect blue bead pieces (figure 1). Connect the last blue bead piece to complete the beaded chain.

fig. 1

3. The oil from your hands might tarnish the new metal charms, so that they are more compatible with the look of the older pieces. Create a slightly distressed look by rubbing the charms with fine sandpaper.

Tools (continued)

Chain-nose pliers, 2 pair

Flat-nose pliers

Round-nose pliers

Wire cutters

Coarse and fine sandpaper

Techniques

Using Jump Rings (page 2)

Rolling Simple Loops (page 3)

Designer's Tips

To bring new life to old brooches, use links from old chains to connect charms and bead dangles. This way, the metals match.

Look for brooches with holes that can be used for jump rings wherever you want to attach charms.

Select beads to match stones in the brooch, so they blend together.

Select a brooch with a theme for which you can find charms easily.

4. Open a jump ring, slide the treble clef charm onto it, and then insert the ring through a brass chain link on the beaded chain. Close the jump ring so it is secure. Attach the music note charm to another brass link in the same manner.

5. Open a jump ring, and connect the end of the beaded chain closest to the treble clef to the bird brooch by closing the jump ring around the tail. Open the remaining jump ring, and connect the loose end of the beaded chain to the nest charm.

Flower Instructions

1. String a crystal bead and bell bead cap onto a head pin, and finish the end of the wire with a loop. Make a second crystal bead dangle in the same manner.

2. String a bead cap, pink glass pearl bead, and bead cap onto the eye pin, and finish with a loop. Open the loop on the eye pin, and connect the leaf charm (figure 2).

fig. 2

3. Open the loop at the top of the leaf dangle and connect it to the center bottom of the flower brooch. Connect the crystal dangles at each side, using the gold jump rings.

NORTHERN LIGHTS

Create dangles to showcase the favorite beads in your stash, and then layer a fine chain swag on top.

NORTHERN LIGHTS

Designer: Stacey Neilson

Finished size: 3¼ inches (8.3 cm)

Materials

20 base metal beads, 2.5 mm

Venetian glass bead (round, flat), 20 mm

Dark green bicone crystal, 6 mm

2 yellow bicone crystals, 4 mm

12 lead-free pewter rondelle spacers with
    fine silver electroplating, 4 mm

Turquoise miracle bead, 8 mm

2 aqua bicone crystals, 6 mm

3 turquoise miracle beads, 4 mm

Venetian glass bead (round), 8 mm

2 aqua bicone crystals, 4 mm

Venetian glass bead (square, flat), 10 mm

2 yellow bicone crystals, 8 mm

Gray miracle bead, 4 mm

Cloisonné tube, 10 mm

Cloisonné drop bead, 17 mm

Crystal teardrop, 12 mm

AB crystal (cushion), 5 mm

Gray round bead, 6 mm

Charm with three holes: one on top,
    two at the bottom, 15 mm

3 lead-free pewter charms with fine silver
    electroplating, 6 to 8 mm

6 head pins, 2 inches (5 cm) long

6 base metal bead caps, 4 mm

(Continued on next page)

Instructions

1. Thread a head pin with a base metal bead, cap, the large Venetian bead, cap, base metal bead, the dark green bicone, base metal bead, small yellow bicone, and base metal bead. Roll a simple loop at the top. Join this to the end link of a ½-inch (1.3 cm) piece of link chain. Attach this dangle to the first loop on the pin with a jump ring.

2. Thread a head pin with a base metal bead, rondelle spacer, turquoise miracle bead, rondelle spacer, 6 mm aqua bicone, rondelle spacer, small turquoise miracle bead, and a base metal bead. Roll a simple loop at the top. Use the simple loop to attach the dangle to the pin's second loop.

3. Make another dangle on a head pin, using a base metal bead, rondelle spacer, Venetian glass round, four rondelle spacers, small aqua bicone, rondelle spacer, and base metal bead. Roll a simple loop and then attach this dangle to the fifth loop on the pin.

4. The last head-pin dangle, which is attached to the pin's sixth loop, is stacked with a base metal bead, cap, square Venetian glass bead, cap, base metal bead, cap, large yellow bicone, cap, base metal bead, small turquoise miracle bead, base metal bead, small yellow bicone, and base metal bead.

5. Cut two lengths of beading chain, each 2½ inches (6.4 cm) long. Pinch a crimp to the end of both of the pieces. Drop a gray miracle bead and small aqua bicone down to meet one of the crimps. A quarter of the way up the length, secure another crimp and then a large yellow bicone. The bead will rest on top of the crimp. Pinch another crimp just above the midpoint, drop on the cloisonné tube. Set aside this chain. On the other length of beading chain, drop on a cloisonné drop bead, pinch a crimp below the midpoint, add a medium-size aqua bicone, then another crimp slightly higher, followed by a small turquoise miracle bead. Place the upper end of both lengths of beading chain into a crimp, and pinch it to secure them. Put the crimp joining these two lengths into the open calotte (figure 1). Pinch the calotte closed with the chain-nose pliers. Add the calotte to a jump ring, and secure this to the fourth loop of the pin.

fig. 1

Materials (continued)

7-hole safety pin brooch, 2¼ inches (5.7 cm)

7 sterling silver jump rings, 4 mm

7 sterling silver crimp tubes, 2 mm

Side-opening sterling silver calotte, 4 mm

Sterling silver jump ring (triangle), 5 mm

5¼-inch (13.3 cm) length of 3 mm link chain

6-inch (15.2 cm) length of 0.8 mm beading chain

Tools

Chain-nose pliers, 2 pair

Round-nose pliers

Wire cutters

Crimp tool

Techniques

Using Jump Rings (page 2)

Rolling Simple Loops (page 3)

Using Crimp Beads and Tubes (page 5)

6. Put the triangular jump ring through the crystal teardrop, and pinch it closed with the chain-nose pliers. Open a jump ring and slip the triangle onto it. Temporarily close the jump ring around the last loop of the pin.

7. The last charm is made by adding two miniature earring-style drops into the lower holes of the three-hole charm. Cut four links from the link chain. Open the link at one end to join this piece to the top hole of this charm. Attach the last link to the remaining available loop on the pin. Make two more dangles that you can attach to the bottom loops of the charm. On one head pin, string a base metal bead, rondelle spacer, cushion crystal, rondelle spacer, and base metal bead. On the other head pin, string a base metal bead, rondelle spacer, large gray round bead, rondelle spacer, and base metal bead. Close both head pins with simple loops, and then use these loops to attach the dangles to the bottom of the charm (figure 2).

fig. 2

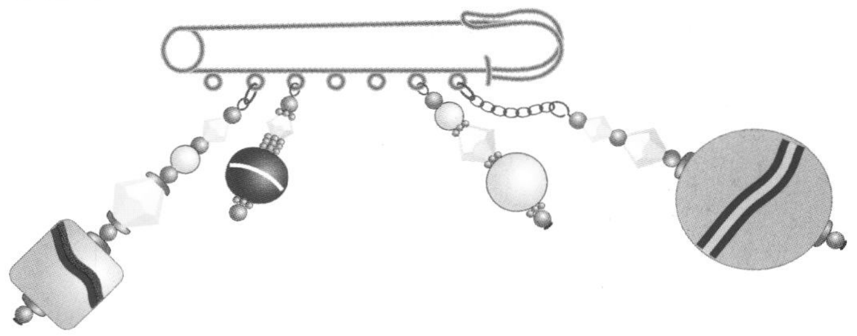

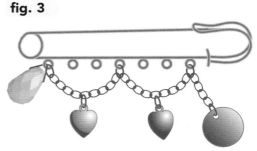

8. Cut a 2½-inch (6.4 cm) piece of chain. Open the triangular jump ring that is attached to loop 7 of the pin. Slip the last link of the chain onto the jump ring.

9. Attach the center of this piece of chain to the fourth loop of the pin, using the jump ring already on that loop. Attach a link near the loose end of the chain to the existing jump ring on the first pin loop, in order to complete the swag. Let the end of the chain dangle below the pin's first loop.

10. Use jump rings to attach a charm to the last link of the dangling end of the chain, and the center of both swags (figure 3).

fig. 3

Bottom layer not shown

ORIENT EXPRESS

Turn your travel memories into jewelry with this eclectic charm bracelet. Anything will work—from game pieces to old coins. A clever extender quickly transforms the bracelet into a necklace.

Instructions

Designer: Candie Cooper

Designer: Candie Cooper
Finished size: 7½ inches (19 cm)

Materials

1 bead for each game piece, 5 mm

Focal beads and pendants, up to 20 mm

Bead assortment, 4 to 20 mm

9 black glass beads (round), 6 mm

8 cinnabar beads (flat hexagon), 16 mm

2 base metal picture frame charms, 17 mm

Base metal charms, 25 to 44 mm

Base metal head pin for each focal bead, 2 inches (5 cm) long

Base metal eye pin for each charm, 2 inches (5 cm) long

2 toggle clasps

2 base metal jump rings, 5 mm

Base metal jump ring for charms and dangle, 5 mm

2 silver crimp beads, 2 mm

7-inch (17.8 cm) length of 10 mm base metal chain

10-inch (25.4 cm) length of base metal 16-gauge 49-strand nylon-coated beading wire

2 pieces of silk fabric or newspaper, or ticket stubs to fit the picture frame charms

Chinese replica coin with center hole, 25 mm

6-inch (15.2 cm) length of silk cord

Game pieces and coins, 22 to 26 mm

Craft glue

(Continued on page 62)

1. Slide interesting pieces of fabric, newspaper, or ticket stubs into the picture frames. Connect these to the chain with a jump ring.

2. Thread the cord through the hole in the coin. Wrap one end around the coin and through the hole again. Add a jump ring and tie the cord ends in a knot (figure 1). Use this jump ring to connect the coin to the chain.

fig. 1

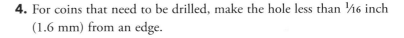

3. Continue making pieces, one for each chain link, and arranging them below the chain as they are completed. Do not attach any more until all of the pieces are finished. This will help you establish attractive spacing between the pieces, as well as ensure that pieces look nice next to each other.

4. For coins that need to be drilled, make the hole less than ¹⁄₁₆ inch (1.6 mm) from an edge.

5. Drill ½ inch (1.3 cm) into the top of each game piece. Thread a 5 mm bead onto a 2-inch (5 cm) piece of wire. Make a simple loop at the end. Trim the wire so the loop butts against the game piece when the wire is inserted in the drilled hole. Dip the end of the wire into the glue, and then insert the wire into the hole (figure 2).

fig. 2

6. Thread each focal bead onto a head pin, and finish with a simple loop or wrapped loop. Place a small charm in the loop of an eye pin, and close the loop. String one to three beads onto the pin, and finish with a simple loop at the top. To make a bead dangle, thread an accent bead onto an eye pin, and finish with a simple loop.

7. Connect the toggle clasp to the ends of the chain with 5 mm jump rings. Attach each piece to the bracelet.

Tools (continued)

Chain-nose pliers, 2 pair

Flat-nose pliers

Round-nose pliers

Wire cutters

Ruler

Scissors

Safety glasses

Drill and #55 drill bit (optional)

Fine-tip permanent marker

Center punch and hammer

320-grit sandpaper

Crimp tool

Techniques

Rolling Simple Loops (page 3)

Making Wrapped Loops (page 3)

Drilling Holes in Metal (page 5)

Using Crimp Beads and Tubes (page 5)

Note: You may not be able to find some of the exact charms shown in the featured piece. These are found objects that have caught the designer's eye. Use the descriptions—and look at the photos—for inspiration so that you can track down your own special finds.

8. For the extender, alternate stringing one black bead and one cinnabar bead onto the beading wire until you have used the last black bead. String a crimp bead onto the wire, followed by a toggle clasp. Put the same end of the beading wire back through the same crimp bead so that ¼ inch (6 mm) extends out the other side. Crimp to secure the wires, and then trim off the excess wire end to finish one end of the extender.

9. Trim the wire 1½ inches (3.8 cm) past the last bead at the opposite end. String one crimp bead onto the wire, followed by the remaining piece for the toggle clasp. Thread the tail of the wire through the crimp bead. Remove all the slack and crimp.

DESIGNERS

Jean Campbell has written and edited more than 45 books, including *Steampunk Style Jewelry* and *Creating Glamorous Jewelry with Swarovski Elements*. A Create Your Style Crystallized Elements Ambassador for the Swarovski Company, she writes a popular blog on www.beadingdaily.com and is the founding editor of *Beadwork* magazine. She teaches jewelry-making workshops throughout the U.S. and on www.craftedu.com. Visit www.jeancampbellink.com.

Bonnie Clewans is an international author, designer, and educator. She has appeared on the DIY Channel and on local television in Buffalo, NY, and Phoenix, AZ. Bonnie has taught at the Bead&Button Show, International Quilt Festival, Bead Expo, Bead Fest, and the Creative Needlework and Sewing Festival. She serves as a consultant to Touchstone Crystal and a Create Your Style Ambassador with Swarovski Elements.

Candie Cooper loves unique materials and color combinations inspired by her years in China. She's the author of *Metalworking 101 for Beaders*, *Felted Jewelry*, and *Designer Needle Felting*. She contributed to many other books as well. She creates designs for craft industry companies, publications, and on-air talent. Candie teaches workshops internationally and has appeared on PBS. Visit www.candiecooper.com.

Erikia Ghumm discovered her love for jewelry making with a dried-macaroni necklace. Since then, she has explored many materials, but still enjoys using found and repurposed items to create distinctive pieces. Erikia is a nationally known scrapbook artist, author, and instructor. Her work has been published in numerous craft magazines and books. See her work at www.erikiaghumm.com.

Tamara Honaman is a freelance designer, writer, and instructor, as well as a certified PMC and Senior Art Clay instructor. She's the founding editor of four publications, including *Step by Step Beads*. She's appeared on PBS and DIY Channel. Find her instructional videos on the *Secrets to Art Clay Success* DVD and through Fire Mountain Gems and Beads, where she hosts "Ask the Experts." Visit www.thonaman.com.

Susan Lenart Kazmer is an award-winning jewelry designer who works in mixed media, found objects, and metals. Her work has been included in museum exhibits throughout the country, including the Smithsonian in Washington, DC; The Art Institute of New York City, NY; and the Huntington Museum of Art, Huntington, WV. *Lapidary Journal* has written that "Kazmer is a pioneer in the field of patination."

Ndidi Kowalczyk is the Education Coordinator for Ornamentea, a bead store in Raleigh, NC. She lives just outside of Raleigh with her husband and two children. In her spare time, Ndidi combines her love of movement, color, and texture to create one-of-a-kind accessories. She also teaches and designs jewelry for her company, hothouse posey.

Linda Larsen explored a range of arts and crafts until she encountered jewelry design and metalworking. From that moment on, she was smitten. Since then, she has been exploring the limitless possibilities. She is the co-owner of www.objectsandelements.com, but spends most of her time working on new products and ideas.

Carol McGoogan discovered quilting and the fiber arts more than ten years ago. Since then, her creative journey has taken her to explore book arts, collage, jewelry making, and metalwork. Her work has appeared in *Cloth Paper Scissors* magazine, and she contributed to *The Adventurous Scrapbooker*.

Marlynn McNutt is the lead jewelry designer for Fire Mountain Gems and Beads. She has created many of the inspirational designs featured on the covers and interior pages of the company's catalogs. She's taught classes for bead shops, small groups, and tours. Marlynn's work has been featured in magazines and books. She has also appeared on the PBS show *Beads Baubles and Jewels*.

Stacey Neilson of Dublin, Ireland, has been beading since she was 12. Her knowledge and design skills came from many areas of the craft: from owning a retail shop to working at bead shows to teaching and writing instructions to designing her own jewelry. Her work has been published in American and British beading magazines and several books.

Beth Taylor is a jewelry designer, metalsmith, and mixed media artist in Bethlehem, PA. Her work gives new life to found objects such as cultural relics, ephemera, hardware, and vintage tin by making such items into quirky yet wearable jewelry. Beth creates jewelry with a sense of meaning, infused with beauty, fun, and funk. Visit www.aquirkofart.com.

Terry Taylor was an author and editor for Lark Books for 15 years. His work included *The Altered Object*, *Chain Mail Jewelry*, *Artful Paper Dolls*, and *Altered Art*. In his new life, he's studying jewelry in the Professional Crafts Program at Haywood Community College.

Andrea Trbovich, owner of www.charmingdarling.com, has loved charm bracelets since she was a child. Her love of charms and her desire to create something artistic and fun led to her website business. Working as an editor by day, Andrea is obsessed with decorating and moonlights as a home stylist. Andrea lives in Hilliard, Ohio, with her two charming children.

Others in the Simply Series